I0467446

High Quality Prints

Original Colorblind Black & White Photography

Decades of being around accomplished artists producing absolutely phenomenal quality work has taught that we are capable of greatness. It is possible to meet our destiny and become it. Experiencing excellence done with such apparent magical ease and humble selfless gratification is the inspiration for this original photography. It is an expression of freedom.

Being colorblind gives an advantage when composing black & white... less confusion. The photos in this collection were selected from thousands of captures. All images were framed in the camera and presented without edits, genuine as seen through the lens. RAW conversion applied by proprietary panchromatic process. Fine art prints available from original files.

info@ BeachNoise.com

Joseph Fleming

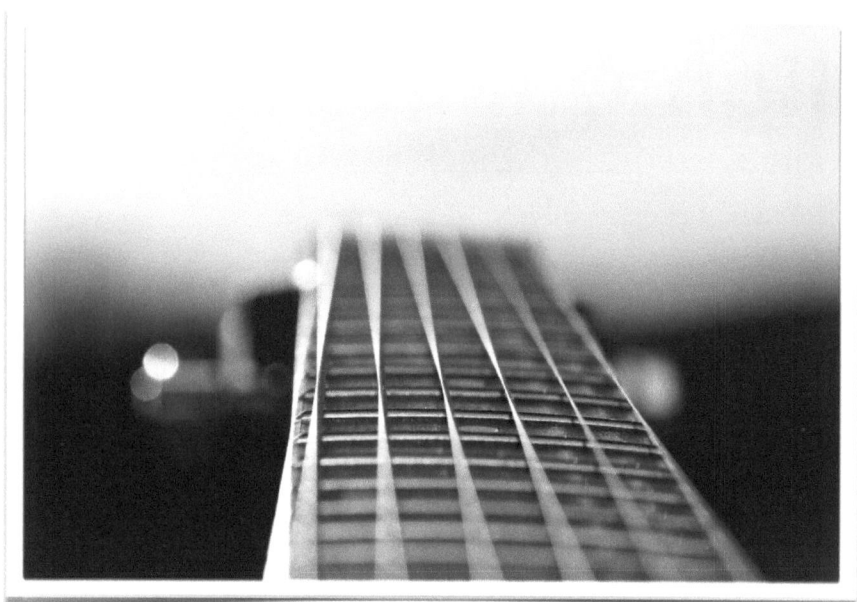

0351

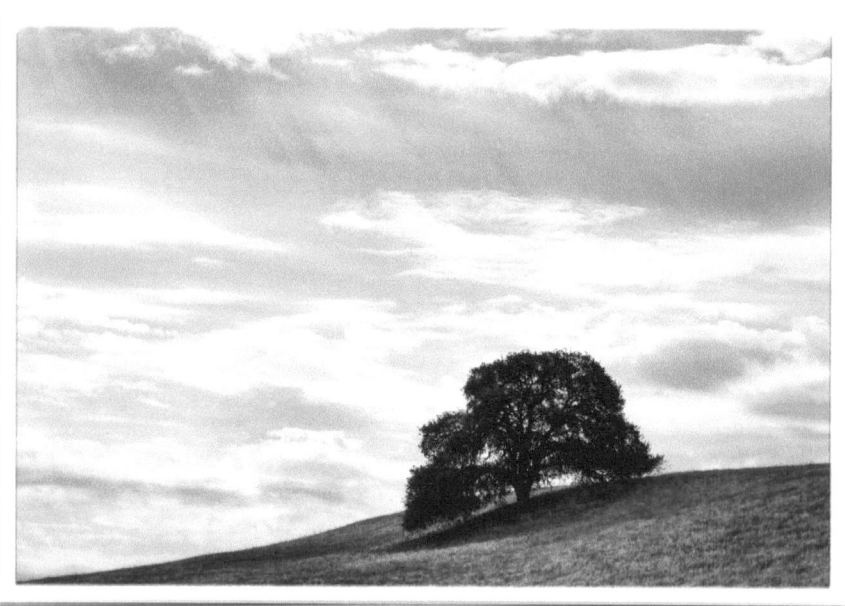

0531

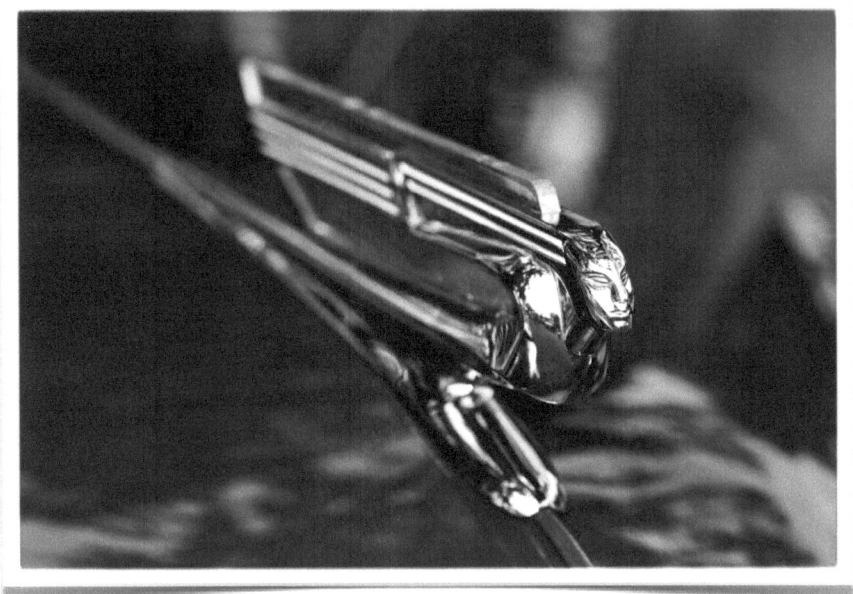

0705

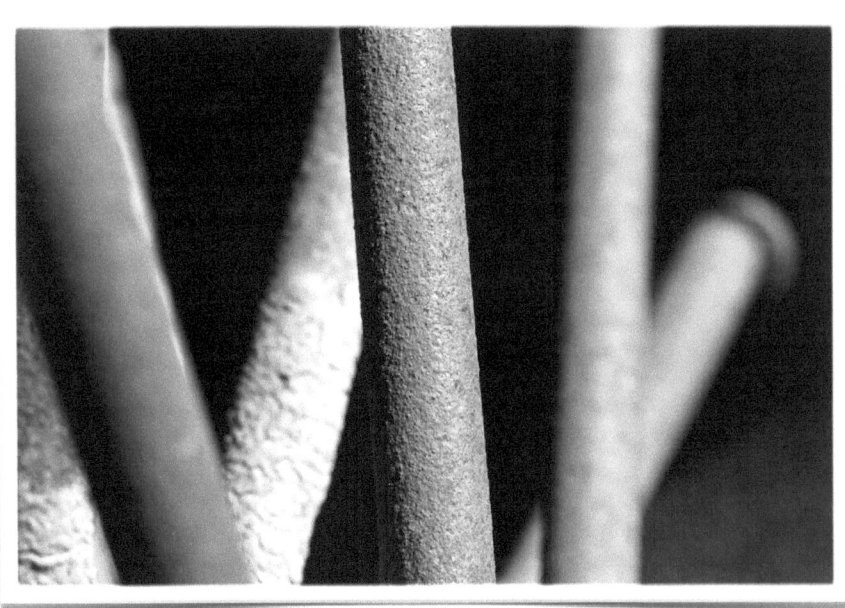

0780

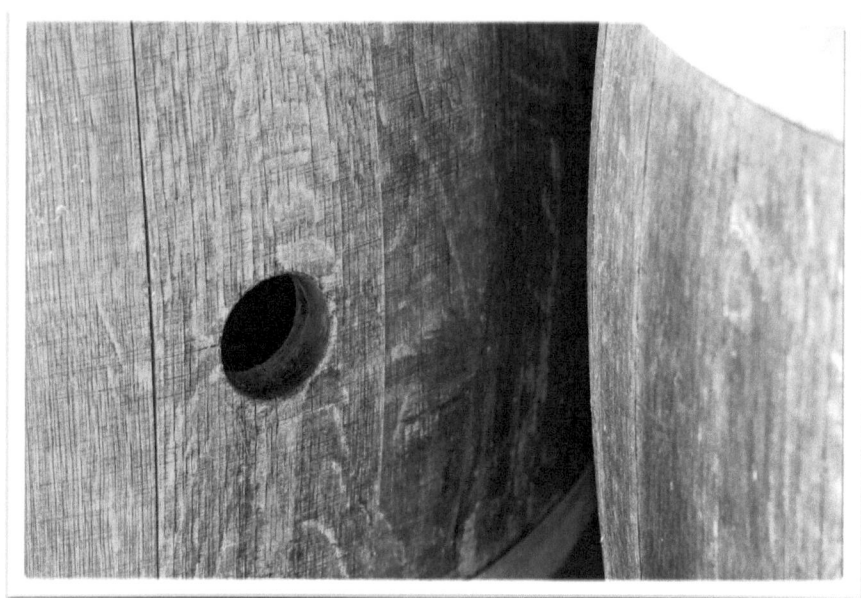

0826

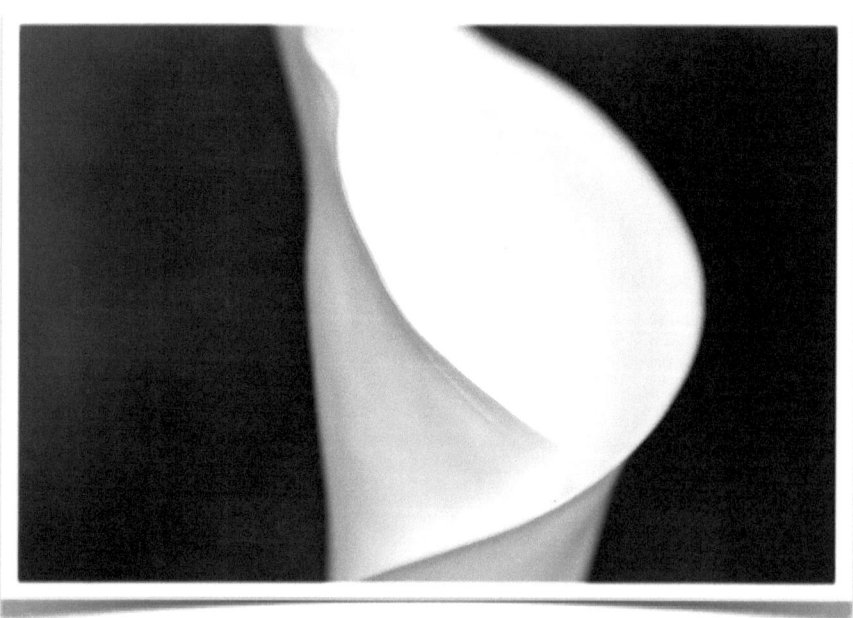

0920

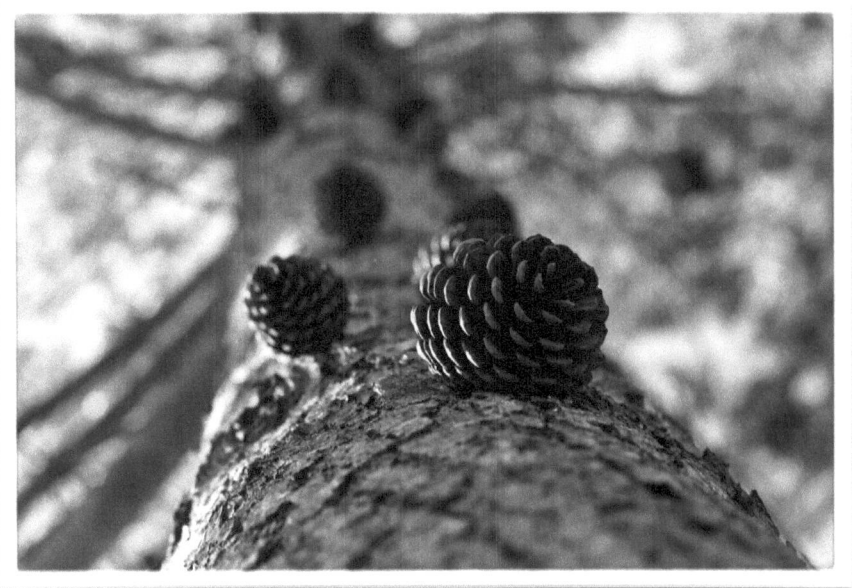

0938

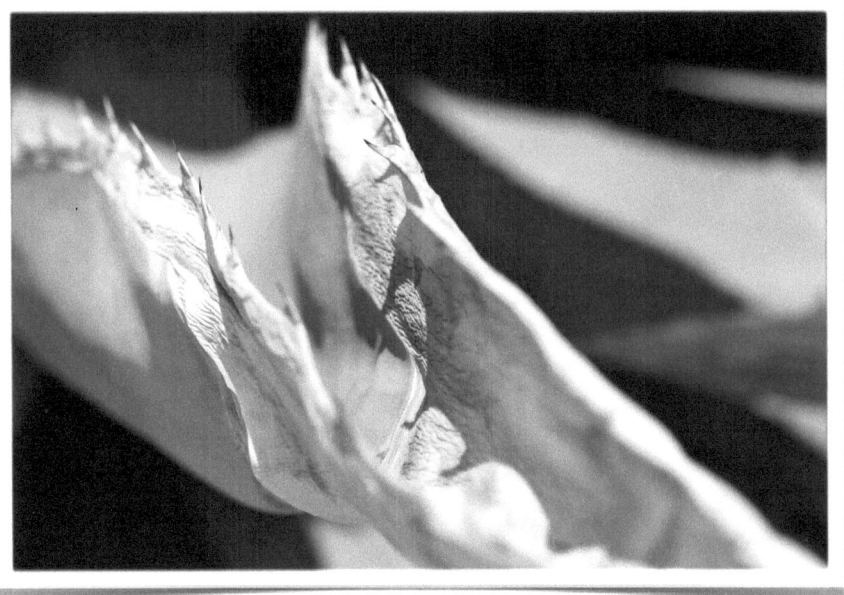

1581

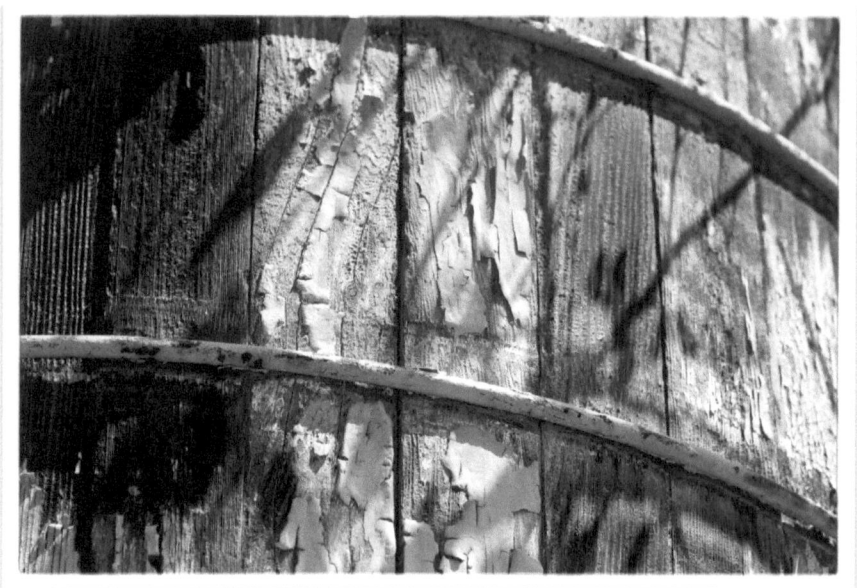

1608

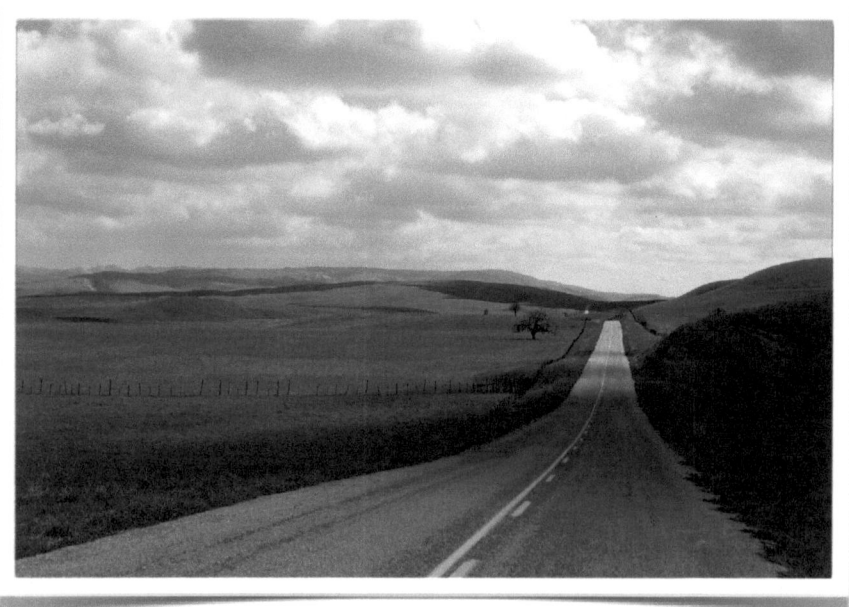

1784

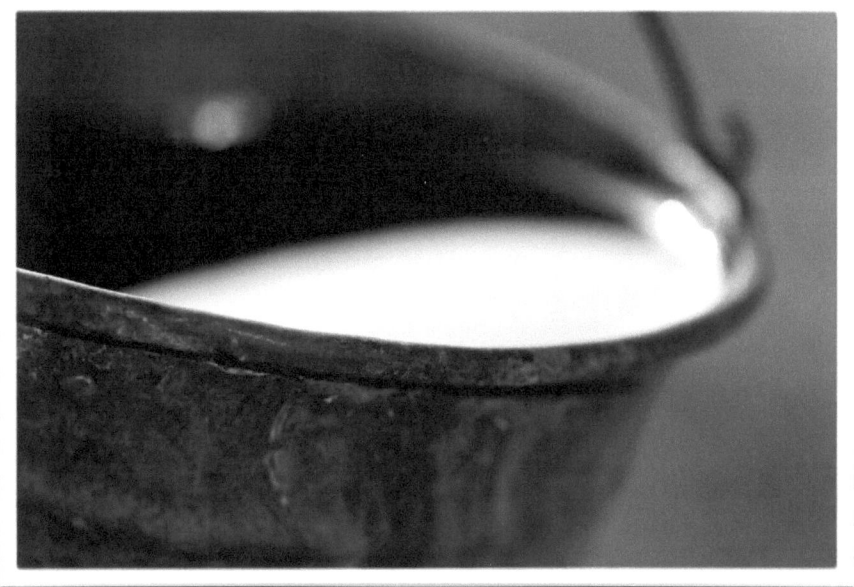

2180

2467

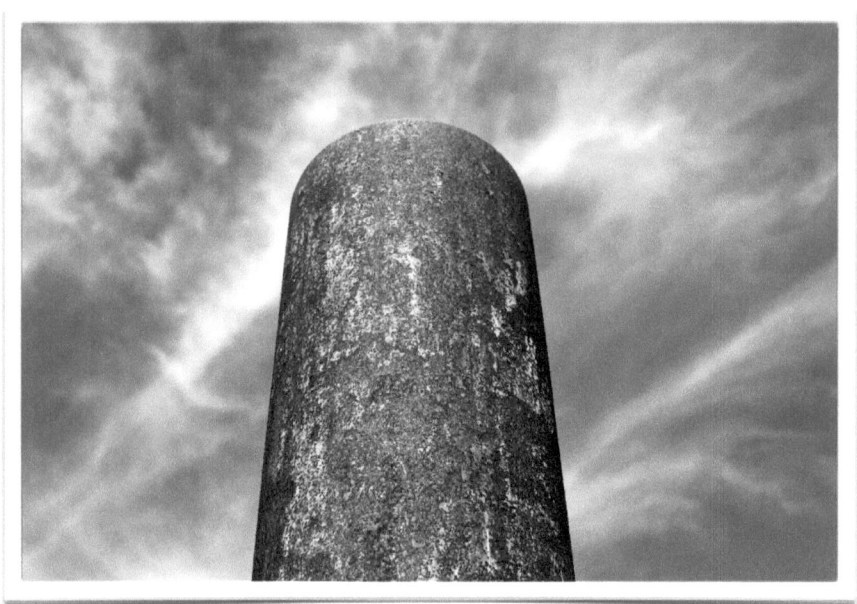

2495

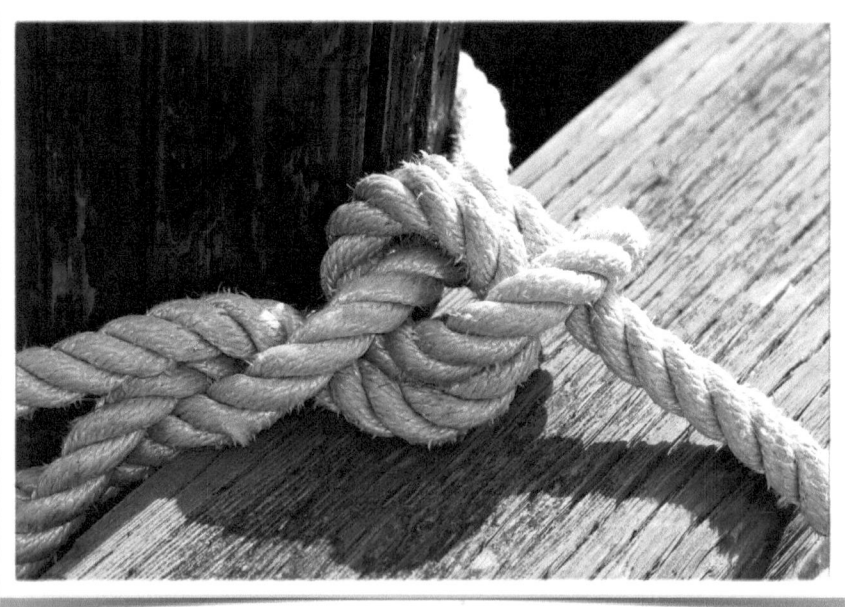

2631

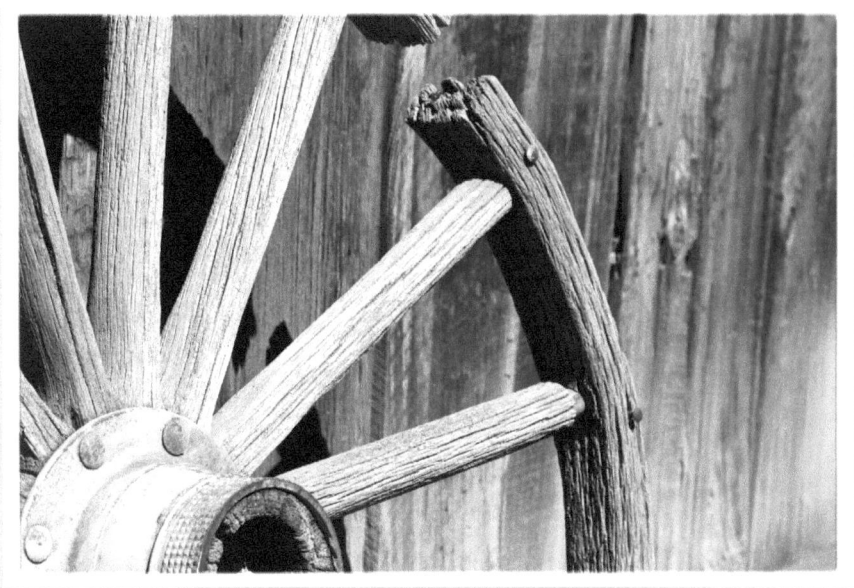

3147

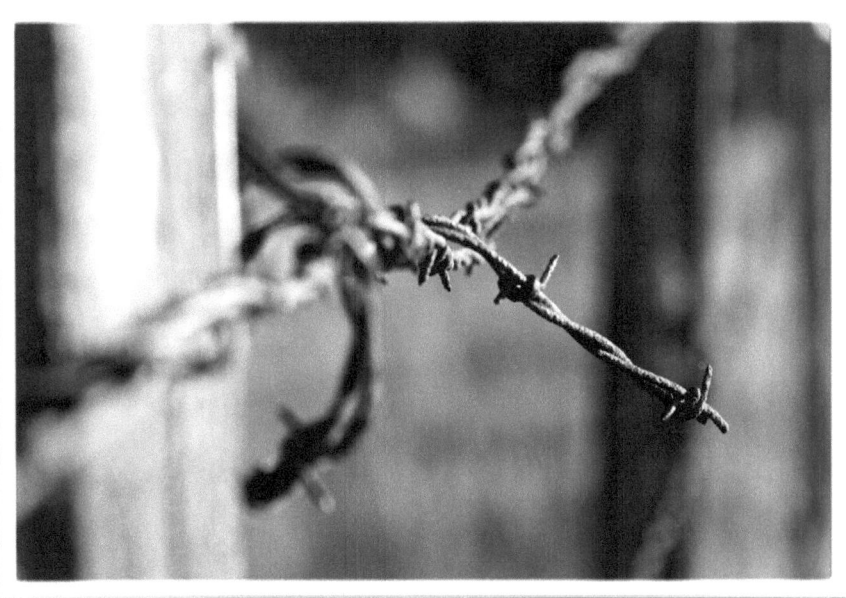

3359

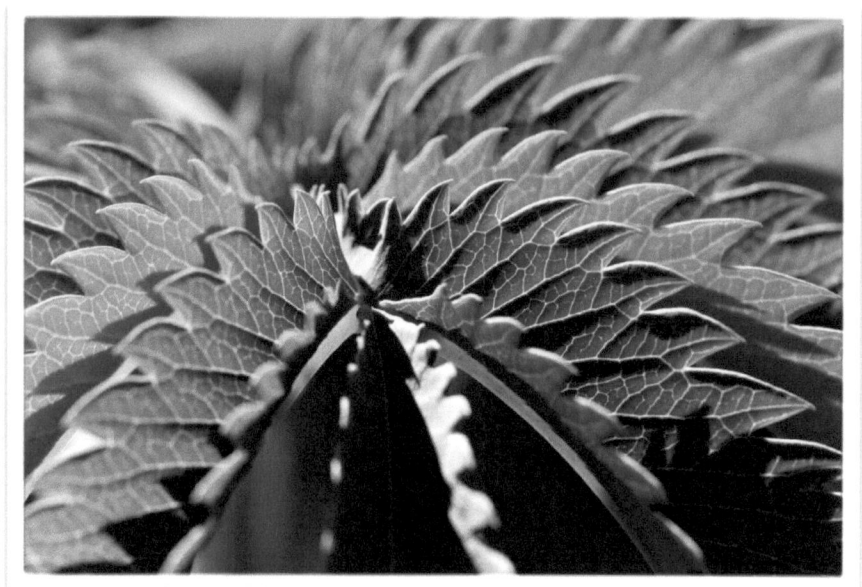

3714

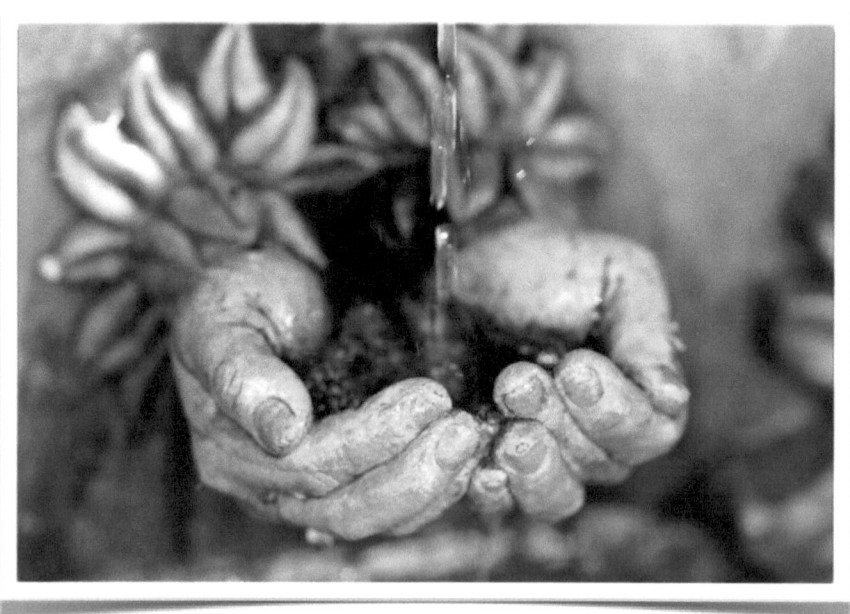

3720

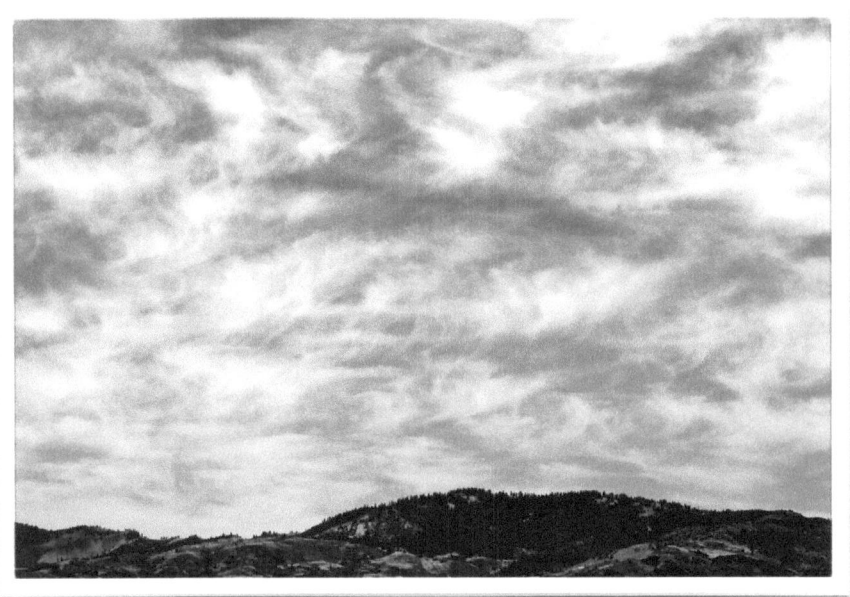

3799

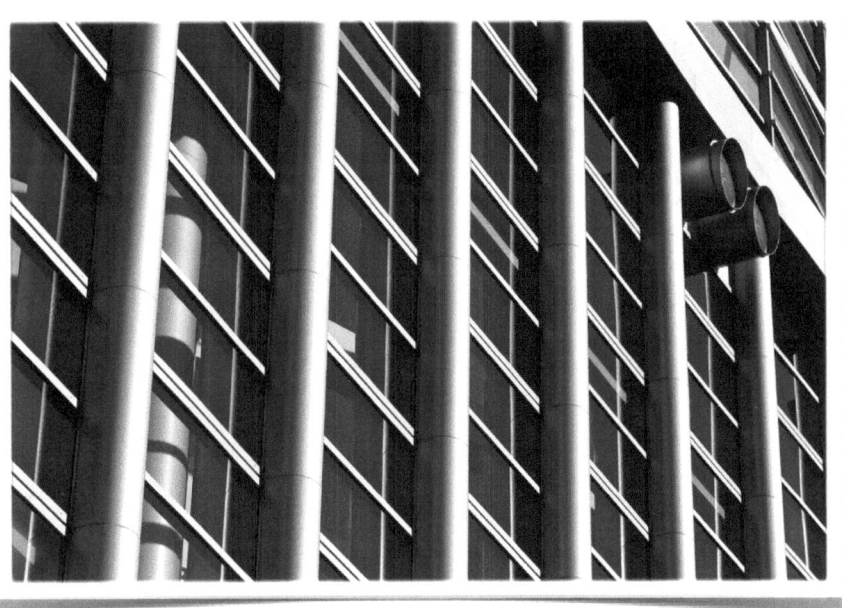

3943

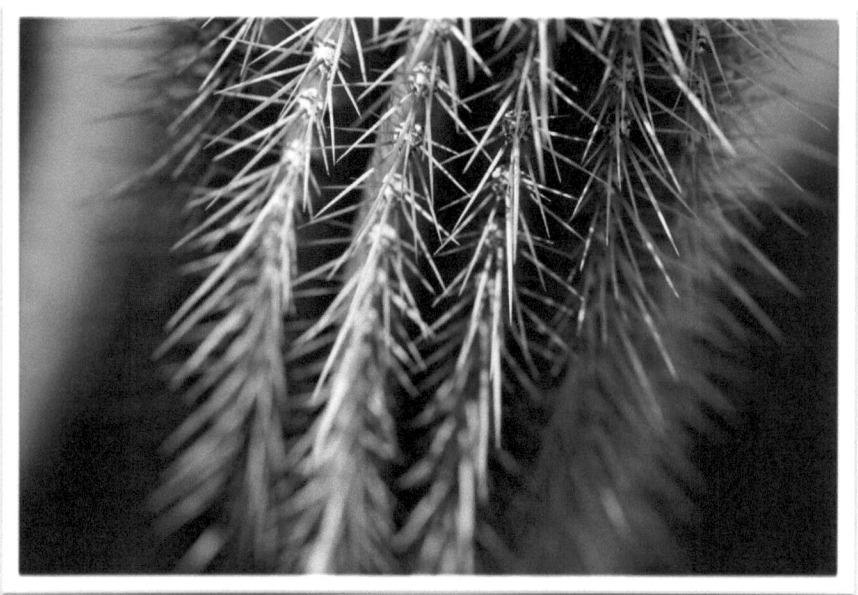

4070

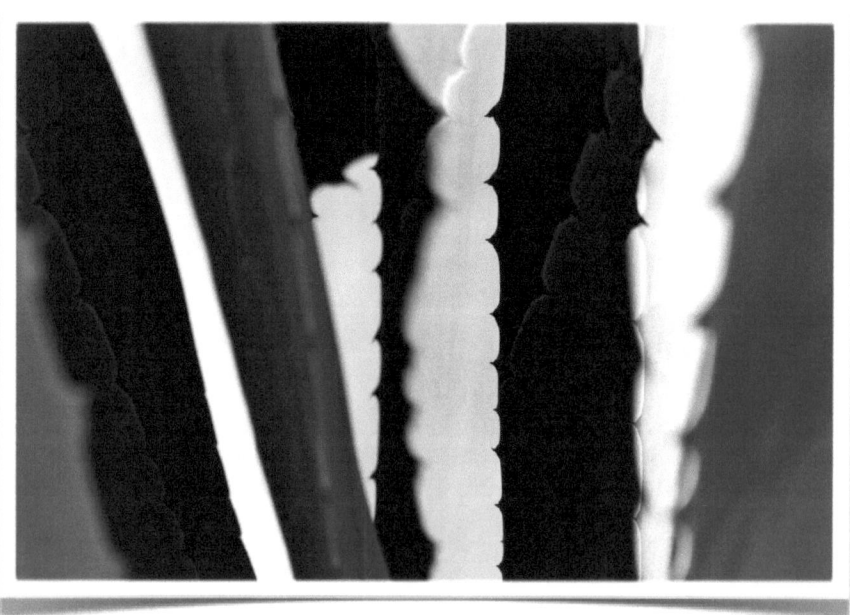

4099

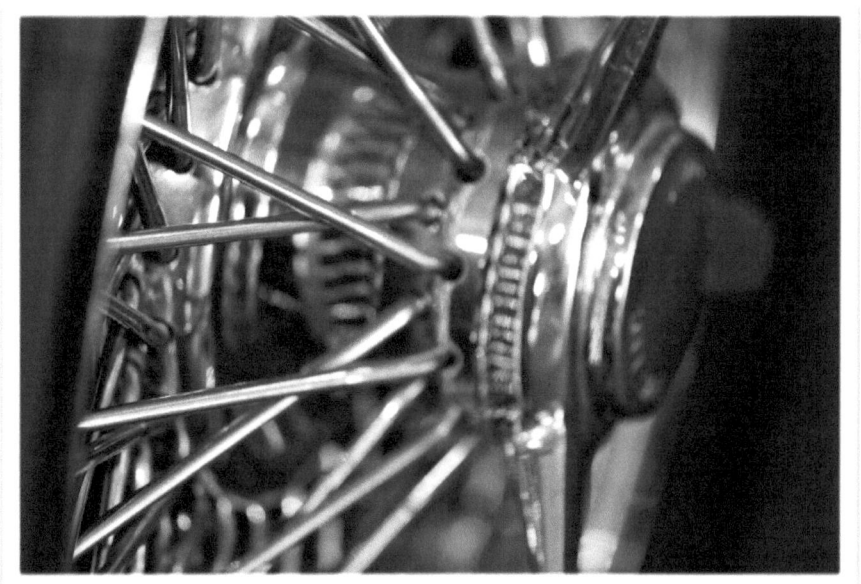

4193

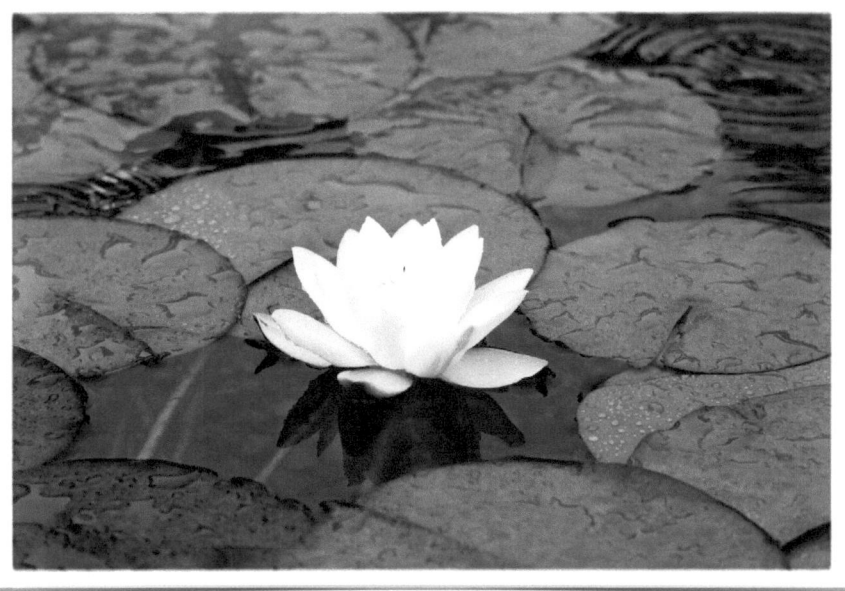

4265

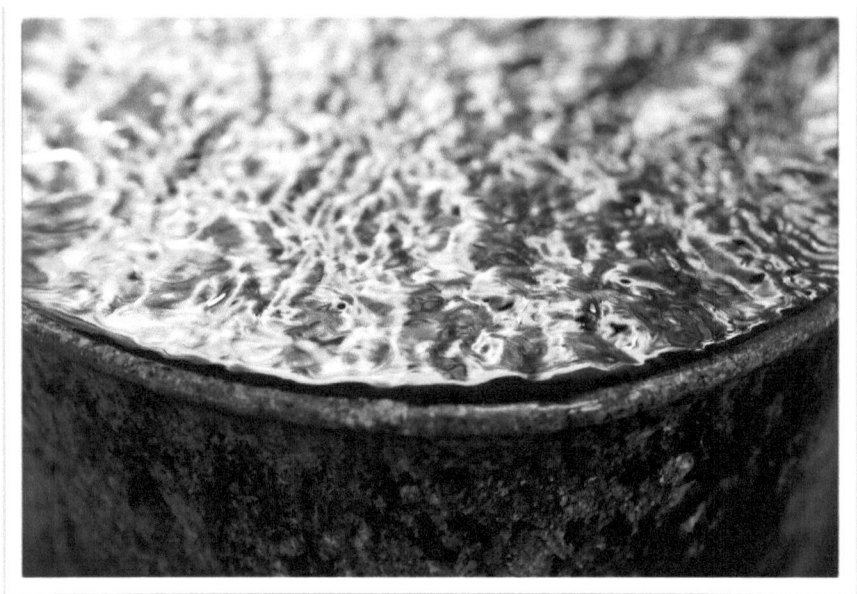

4533

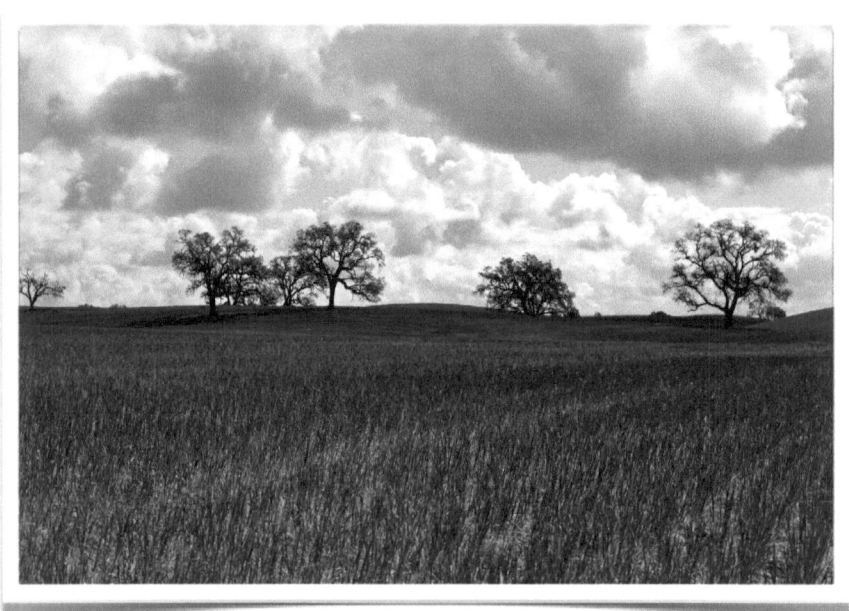

4879

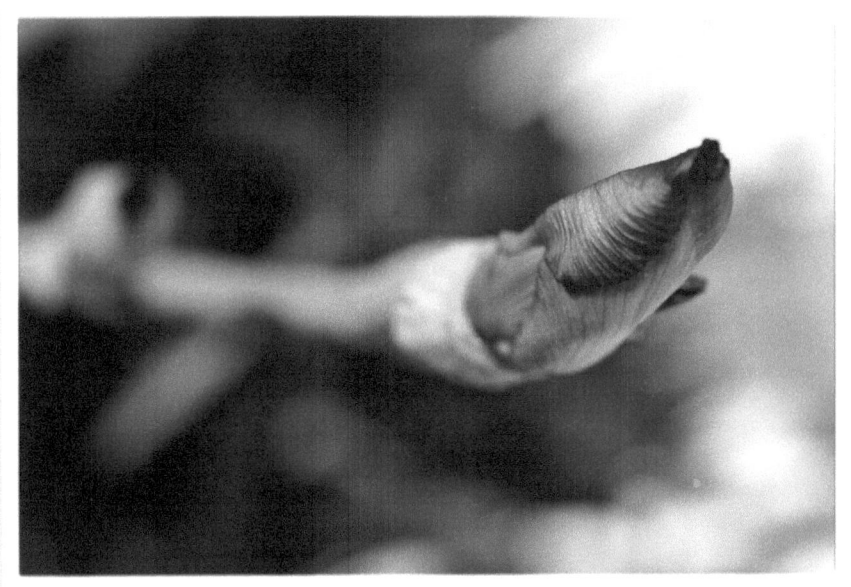

5492

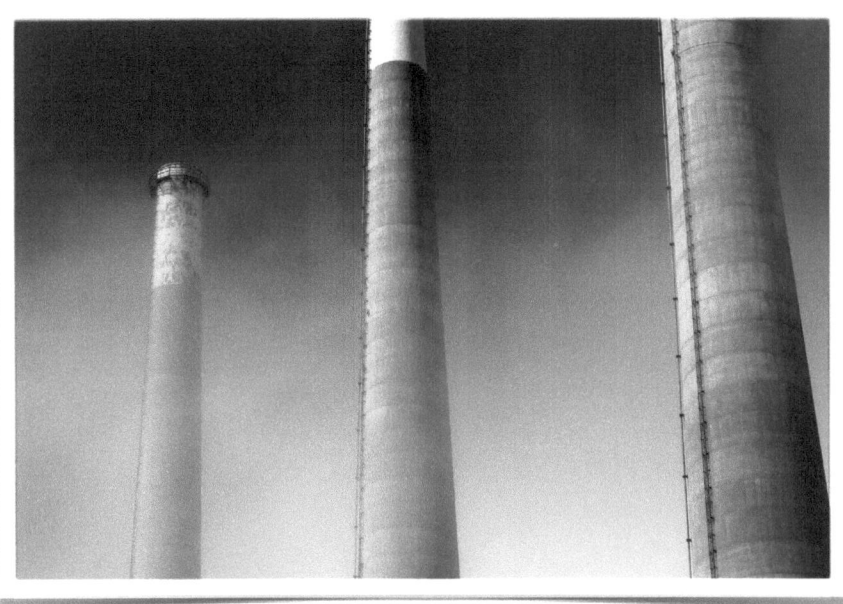

5541

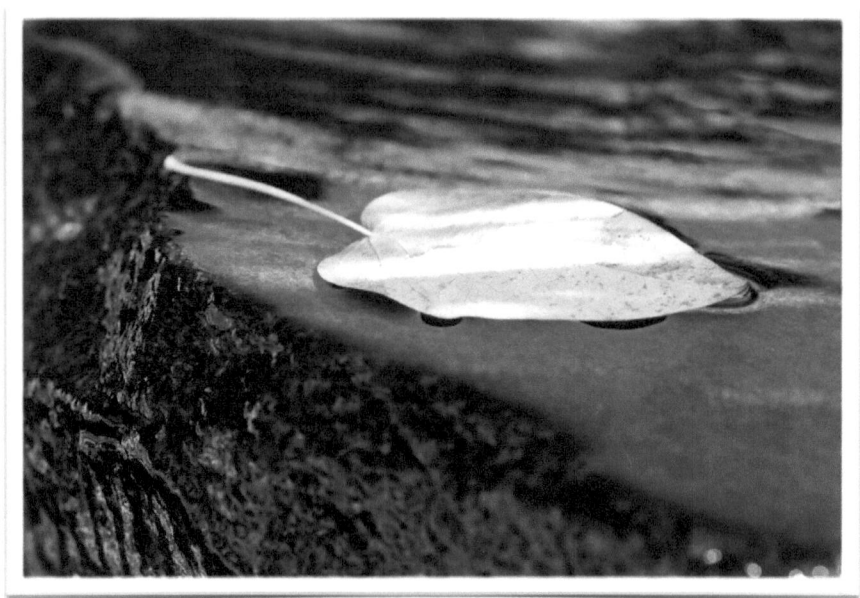

5750

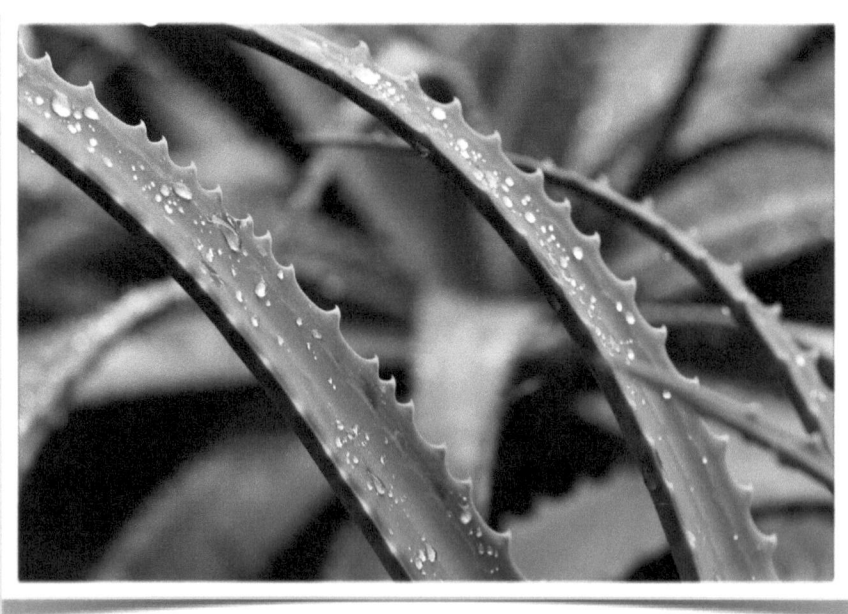

5784

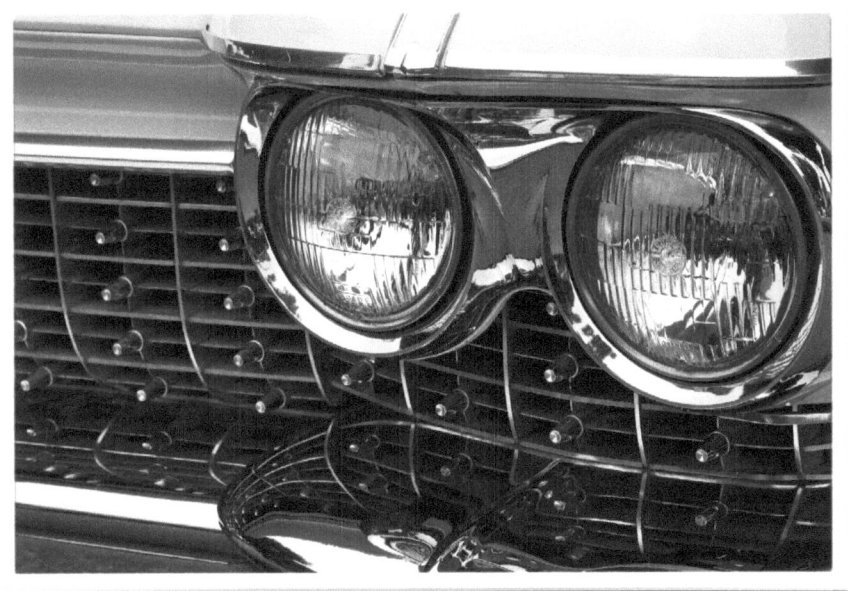

5844

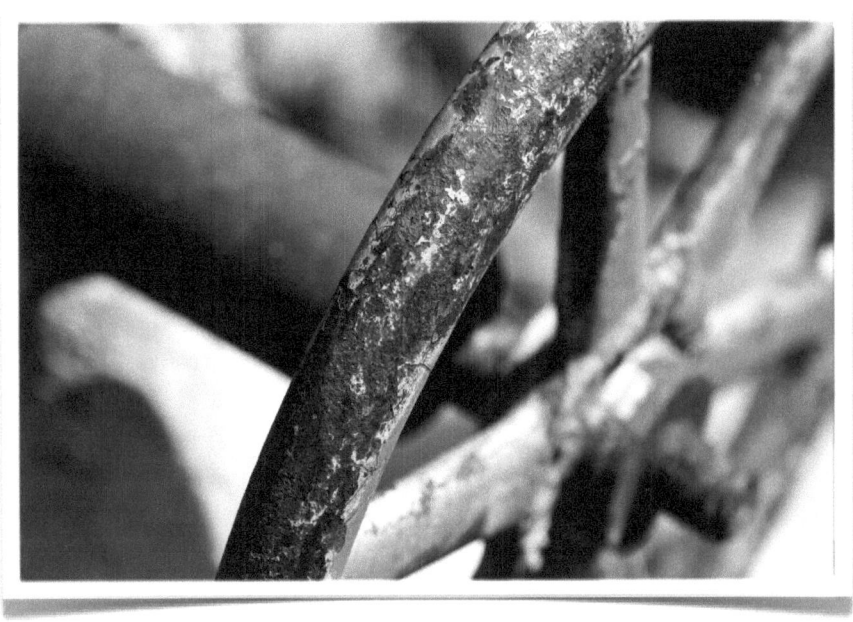

6095

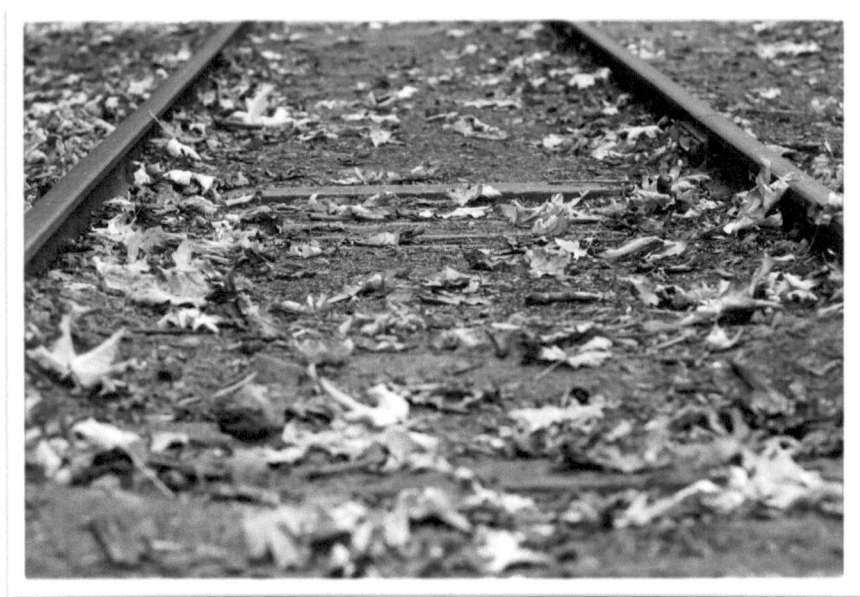

6176

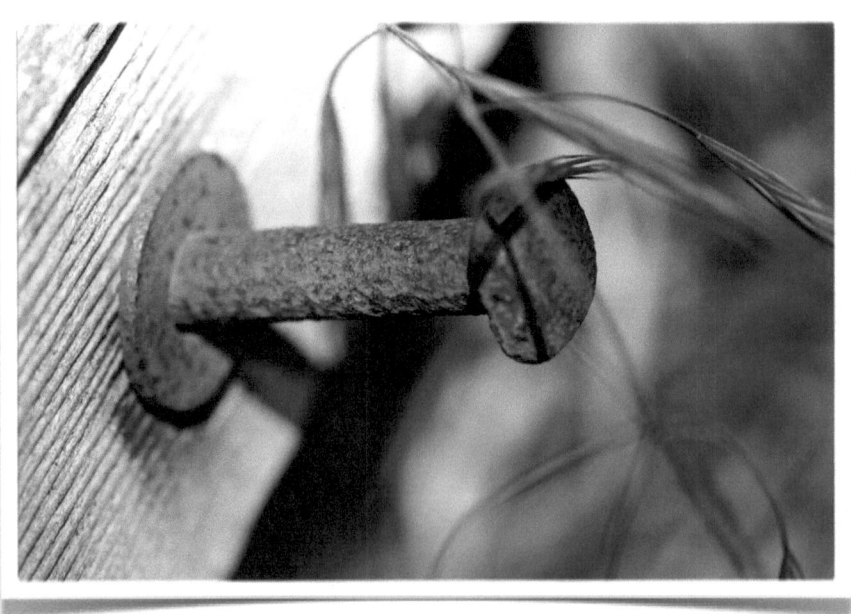

7182

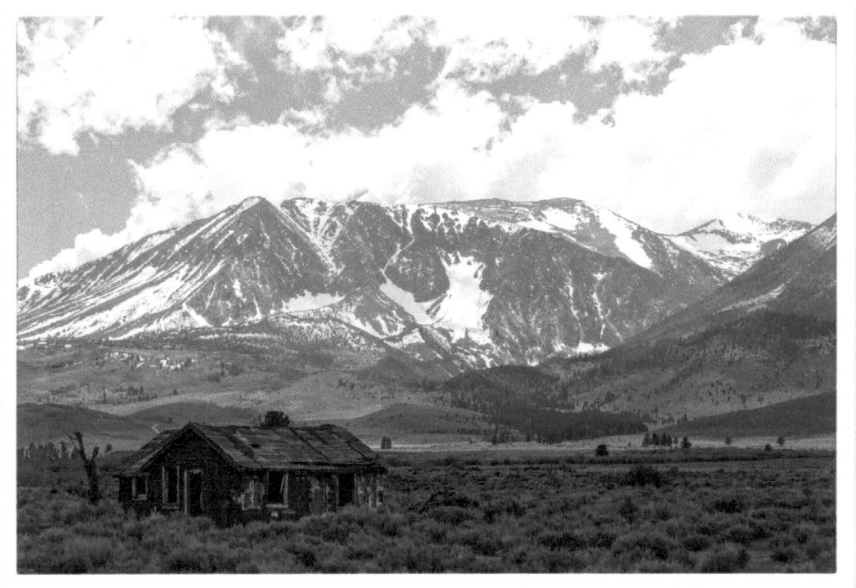

7339

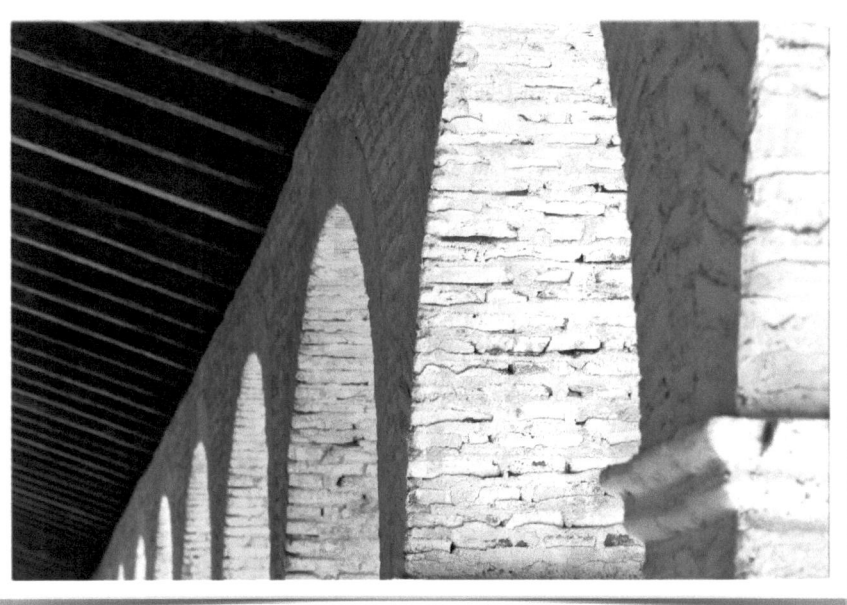

7656

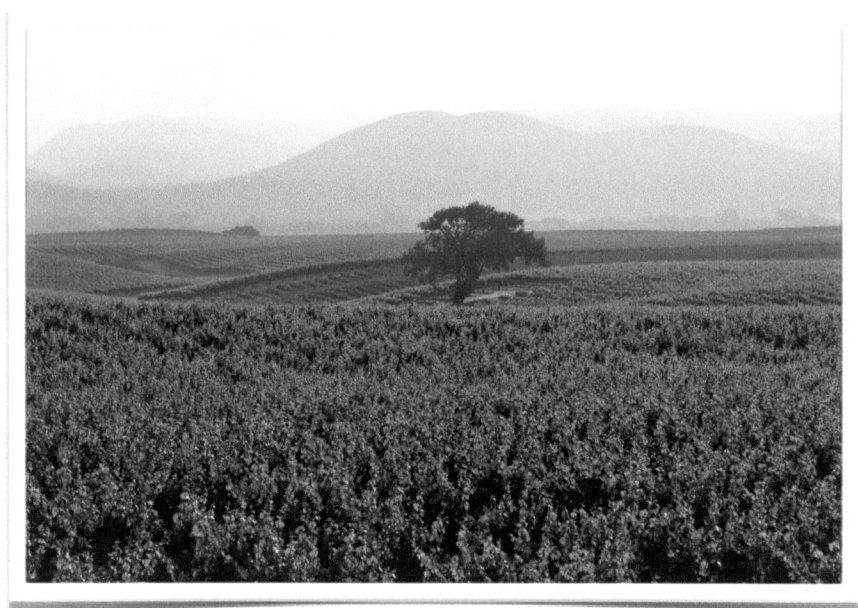

7939

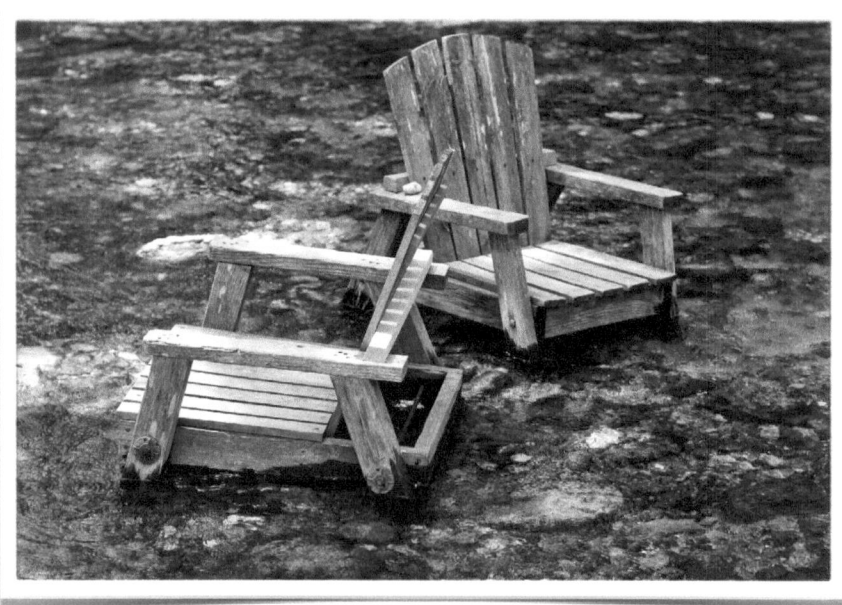

8173

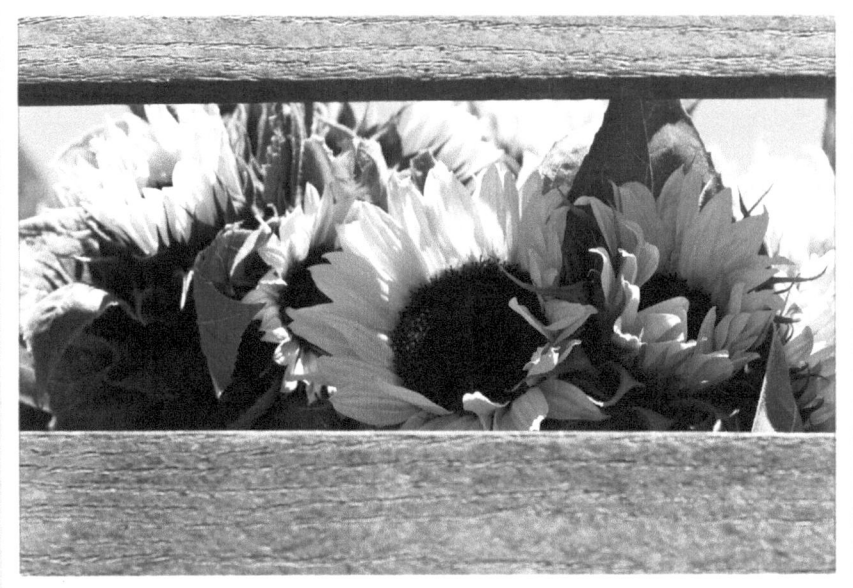

8345

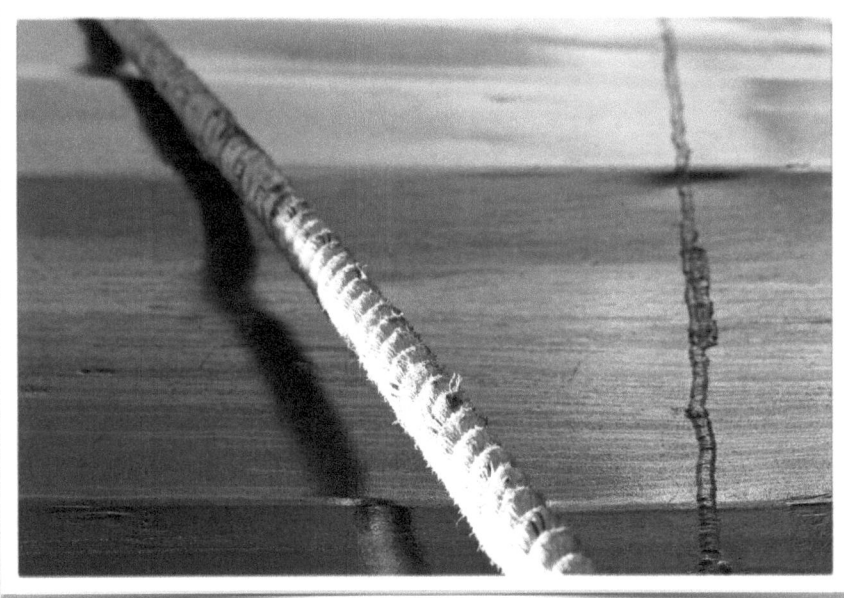

8470

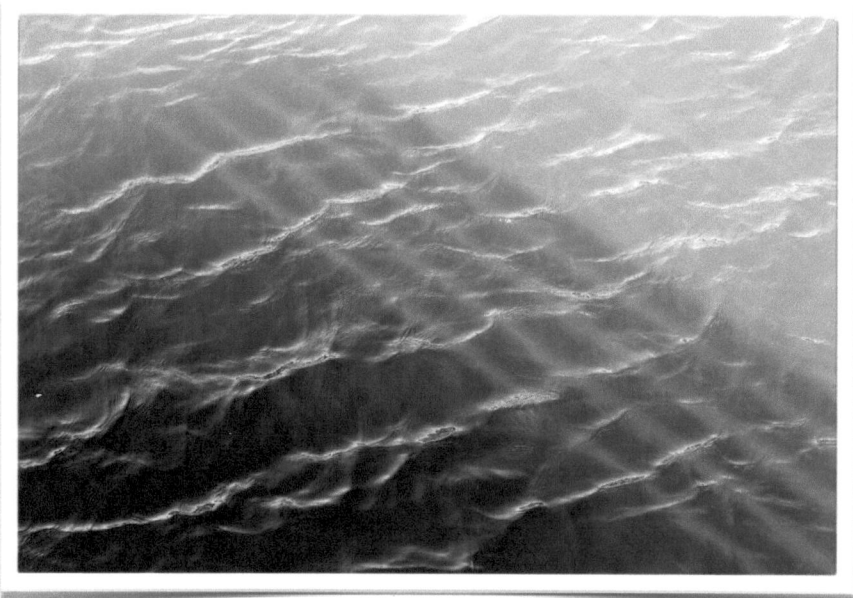

8471

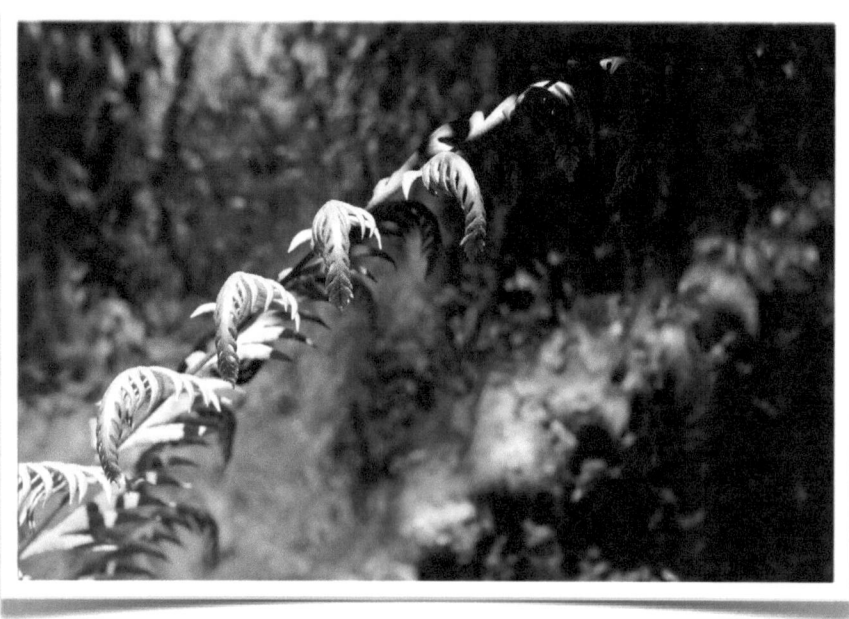

8889

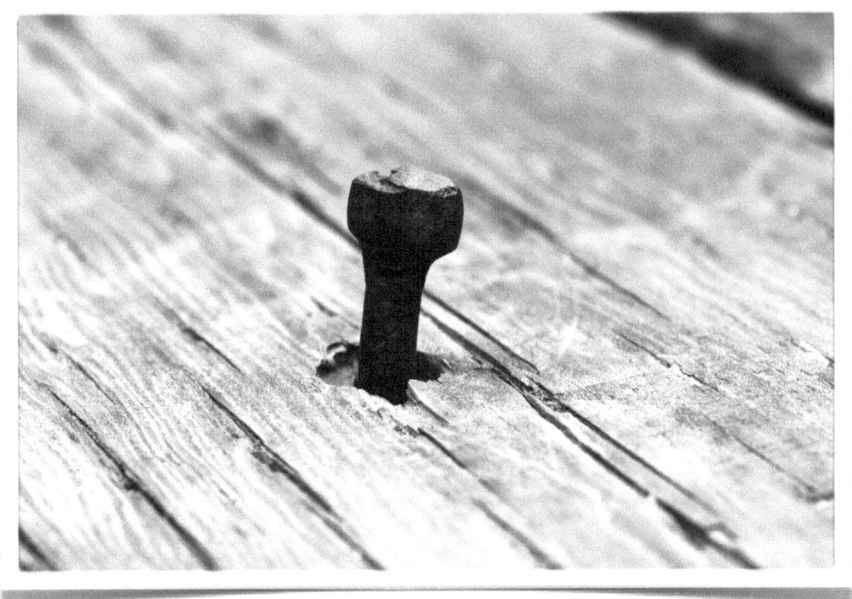

9024

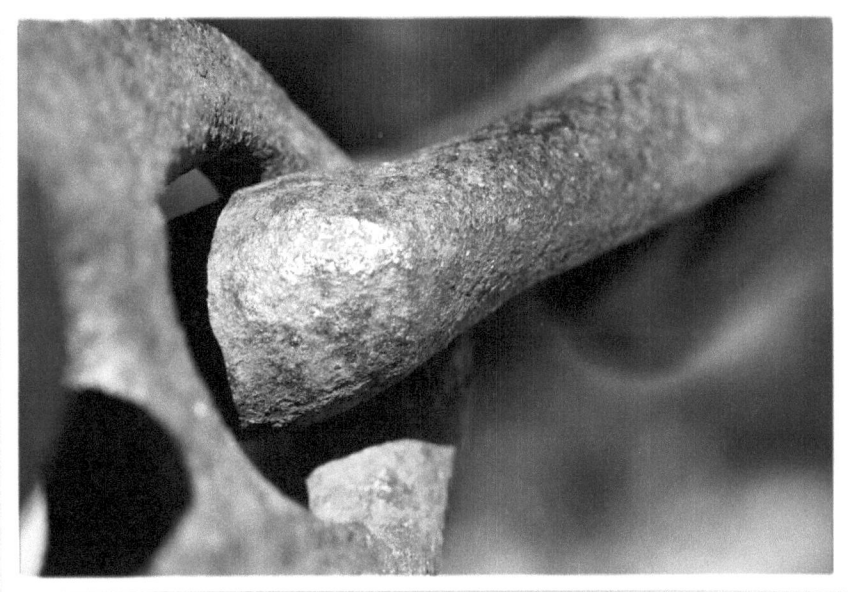

9353

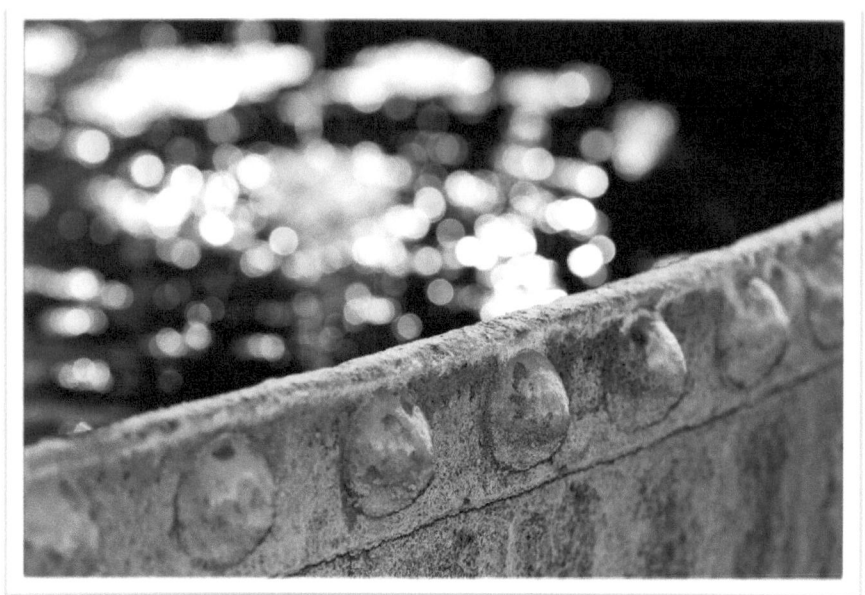

9430

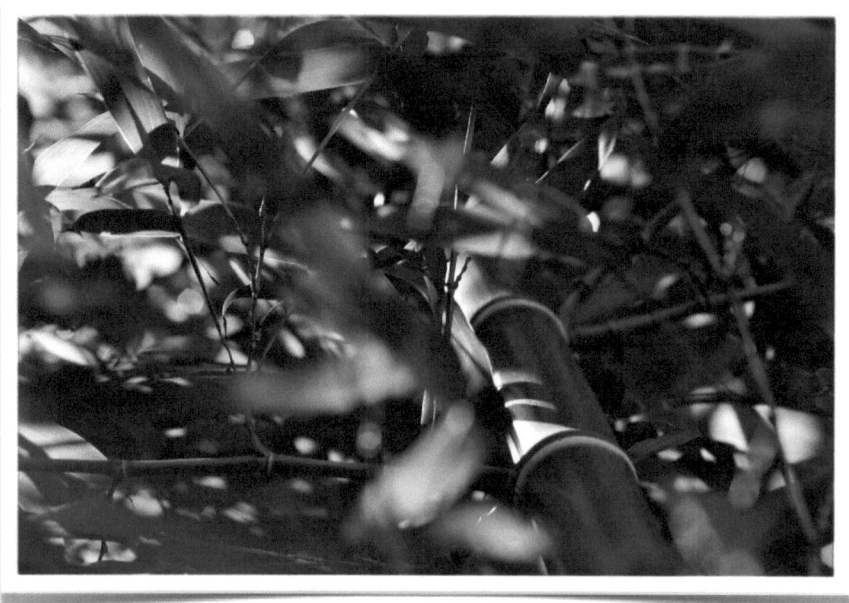

9975

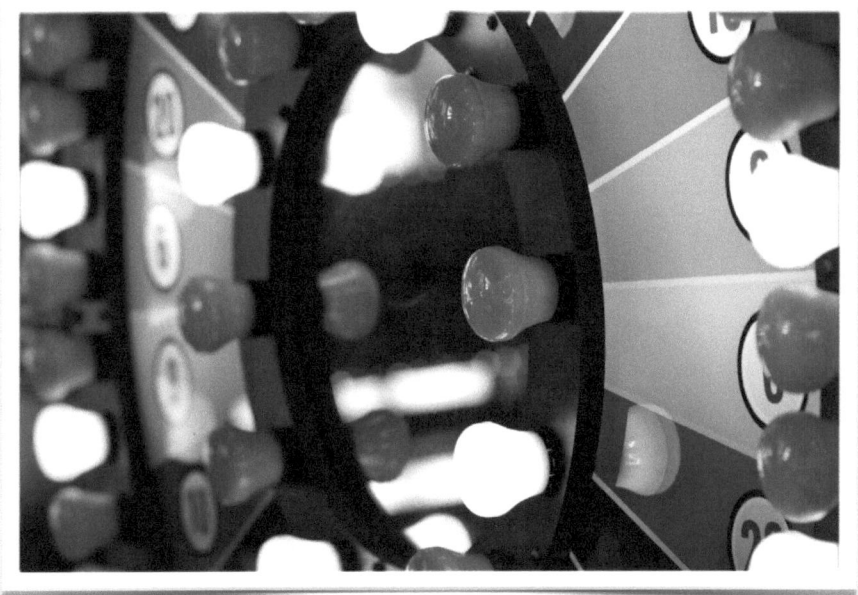

9980

9992

www.ingramcontent.com/pod-product-compliance
Lightning Source LLC
Chambersburg PA
CBHW041620180526
45159CB00002BC/950